Tie-Dyeing and Batik

Tie-Dyeing and Batik

Octopus Books

Editorial production by
Berkeley Publishers Ltd.

First published 1974 by
Octopus Books Limited
59 Grosvenor Street, London W1

ISBN 0 7064 0320 7

© 1974 Octopus Books Limited

Produced by Mandarin Publishers
Limited
14 Westlands Road, Quarry Bay,
Hong Kong

Printed in Hong Kong

Introductory instructions by
Fatidjah Anderson

Tie-Dye:
all by Mary Frame
of Mary Frame Workshop, London.
all dyes by Dylon
additional techniques by Marion
Thurston

Batik:
all by Helen Anstey
except Table Cover by Rosalyn
Anderson
and make-up for Long Dress by
Lydia Cole-Powney
Javanese Batik courtesy of Lydia
Cole-Powney

*Frontispiece: Flower Head design, using
tied circle technique.*

Contents

Tie-dyeing

Batik

Introduction

Tie-Dye and Batik designs are achieved by the resist dyeing process – that is, only the exposed part of the fabric "takes" the dye. Yet each has its own unique basic methods that are easily mastered.

The variations for both are truly endless for both design and colour. In working, one can be spontaneous and quick, meditative and slow. It all depends on the mood – and the person – for these techniques may be used by young and old, beginner and experienced.

Within the past few years these arts, which have been kept alive for centuries in the East, have found a new home in the West, where tie-dye and batik enthusiasts have contributed an individual spirit to the techniques.

In this book, we swing easily from East to West, borrowing processes and some motifs but adding, too, our own discoveries.

We start you off with step-by-step instructions for simple and more complicated designs, with colour illustrations of the finished articles – from a simple wall hanging to a long flowing gown.

The rest we leave to your own imaginations. . . .

Garment Sizes

All adult garments are cut to a generous size. Follow the measurements in the make-up diagrams but adjust during make-up to your own requirements.

History of Tie-Dyeing

Tie-Dyeing, which is simply a method of tying or stitching fabric together to prevent absorption of the dye, had a mysterious beginning. Research has uncovered that the art touched many cultures and that this technique was of natural origin in several areas and cannot be traced to one particular place.

It is known that Tie-Dyeing existed in China during the T'ang Dynasty (618–906 A.D.) and in Japan in the Nara period (552–794 A.D.). The tradition is also indigenous to and has existed for centuries in Southeast Asia, Indonesia and India, in addition to Peru and parts of Africa.

The discovery of synthetic dyes and their subsequent improvement encouraged even more widespread use of the technique, which is reaching the height of its popularity all over the world today.

Colour and Dyeing Tips

If you are using two or more colours for your article, they will, of course, blend with each other. (Also, the amount of time you leave the fabric in the dye will affect the final colour.) Successive dyeings result in a steady build-up of dark colour on the areas left exposed. Before starting your piece, you might like to experiment on a small bit of fabric to see if you attain the desired effect.

Remember the basic rules of colour mixture:

Red	+	**Yellow**	=	**Orange**
Red	+	**Blue**	=	**Purple**
Yellow	+	**Blue**	=	**Green**
Purple	+	**Green**	=	**Grey**
Purple	+	**Orange**	=	**Brown**
Violet	+	**Blue**	=	**Indigo**

As tie-dyeing has so many colour combinations and possibilities, it is a good idea to keep a notebook for jotting down your own discoveries.

Types of Dyes

For the sake of uniformity and ease of instruction, we've used Dylon dyes for the articles made especially for this book. However, other brands are equally suitable. Dylon (and, generally, other dye manufacturers) produce the following types of dyes:

Cold Dyes Very easy to use in cold or warm water. For each colour, use 1 container for 6–8 ozs. of dry fabric (approximately 2–3 sq. yds. of medium weight fabric). For example, a 1 lb. dress for tie-dyeing in blue and red needs 2 containers of blue and 2 of red.

Multi-purpose Dyes Can be used in hot water. Simmering gives greater density of colour. For each colour, use 1 container for $\frac{1}{2}$ lb. of dry fabric (2–3 sq. yds. of medium weight fabric).

Liquid Dyes Convenient version of Multi-purpose dyes. Comes in plastic bottle to dye up to 2 lbs. dry fabric (8–10 sq. yds. medium weight fabric).

In the "Method" for each tie-dye article we have mentioned the particular colour of dyes used to achieve the result in the picture. You could of course use other colour combinations to achieve different results of your own choosing.

Fabric Guide

Cotton or Linen Either Cold, Multi-purpose or Liquid dye. Choose Cold dye for towels, sheets, pillowcases, tablecloths and anything else that is washed often.

Cottons with special finishes Cold dyes in strong colours will give paler results.

Silk Either Cold, Multi-purpose or Liquid (Multi-purpose and Liquid give richer shades on silk).

Rayon Cold, Multi-purpose or Liquid.

Polyesters Triple-strength Multi-purpose or Liquid.

Polyester/Cotton Mixtures Cold, Multi-purpose or Liquid (use Cold for shirts and often-laundered items).

* If you want a strong colour effect, use more dye than recommended.

Dyeing Technique

These general step-by-step instructions can be followed, with slight variations, for any article you plan to tie-dye. Although we have chosen a particular technique (tied circles, using Cold Dye) to illustrate the steps, any other technique may be substituted. Also included are slightly varied instructions for Multi-purpose and Liquid dyes:

Cold or Warm Water Method *(Cold Dyes with Cold Fix)*	**Hot Water Method** *(Multi-purpose or Liquid Dye)*

1a. Wash and iron material to be dyed. Usually new cotton has some finish on it, so boil with soap powder. Dry thoroughly, unless you wish colours to merge. Then leave slightly damp.

1a. Same as Cold Dye.

1b. Choose a large container for submerging the garment – a bowl, bucket, sink, or your washing machine.

1b. If you decide to simmer to get greater density of colour, a heat-resistant container must be used.

1c. Assemble materials:
Cold Dyes
Cold Fix or household soda
Rubber gloves
Kitchen salt
Spoon for stirring
Jug to hold 1 pint
Thread, string or elastic bands for binding
Scissors
Sharp knife

1c. Same as Cold Dye, except for substitution of Multi-purpose or Liquid Dyes for Cold Dyes and Cold Fix.

Cold or Warm Water Method

2. Bind the fabric. For circular pattern, pull material up towards the centre like a closed umbrella and bind downwards at intervals. Thread is run on from one solid band of binding to the next before being knotted off. If you wet the bound areas before dyeing, the inner areas of the material will remain white and give sharper definition to pattern.

3. Prepare the dye, wearing rubber gloves. Generally, use lightest colour first. Pierce the container(s). Dissolve contents of each in 1 pint warm water. Dilute with cold water. Stir well and pour into dyeing container. For each container of dye, dissolve 4 heaped tablespoons of salt in dye solution. Dissolve 1 packet of Cold Fix (or 1 heaped tablespoon of household soda) in 1 pint hot water. Stir well and add to dye. Immerse sample for about 1 hour, stirring occasionally. Remove.

4. Wash in boiling detergent solution, then rinse well until water is clear and dry out on folded newspaper. (Thorough washing and rinsing removes all loose dye particles.)

5. When dry, untie. Second colour may now be dyed over the first, once you have re-tied.

6. Re-tie. Add central bindings, and bind each of the four corners. Prepare the next dye and dye as in 3.

7. When sample is dry, untie and iron.

8. Finished sample, mounted on cardboard, makes an unusual wall decoration.

Hot Water Method

2. Same as Cold Dye.

3. Dissolve powder in 1 pint boiling water, stirring well. Stir in 1 heaped tablespoon of salt for each container. Add this dye to the minimum amount of very hot water to cover article. Immerse for 15–20 minutes, stirring occasionally. Or, simmer over heat for 20 minutes.

4. Rinse until water is clear.

5. Same as Cold Dye.

6. Same as Cold Dye.

7. Same as Cold Dye.

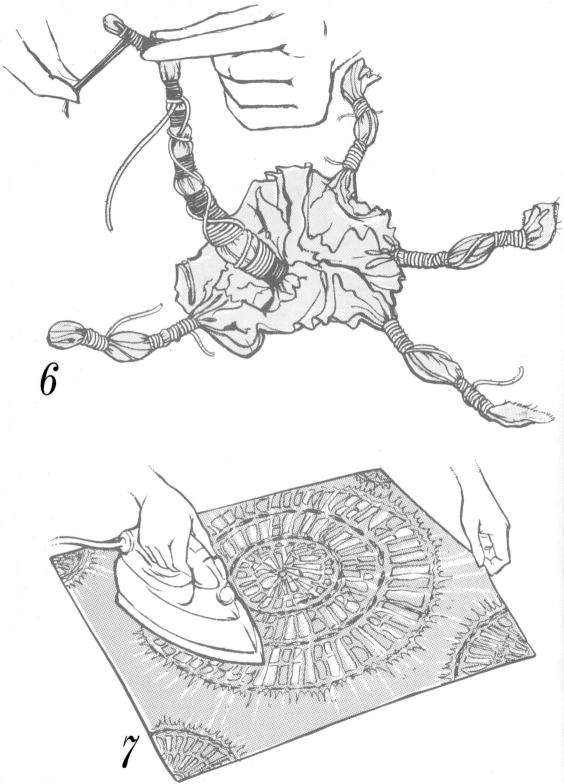

6

7

Here is the finished pattern obtained from the technique we have been showing you.

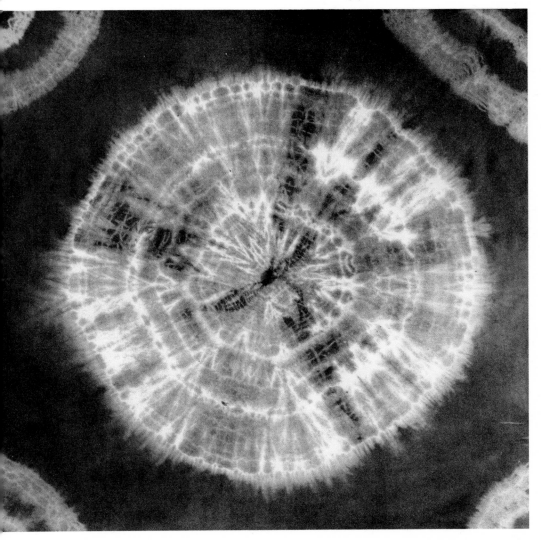

Kimono

Technique
Tied Circles

Materials
1. Fine string.
2. $3\frac{1}{2}$ yds. pure silk × 36 ins. wide.
Dyes: Bahama Blue, Lilac, Purple Vine, Leaf Green

Method
First Tie
1. Cut silk crosswise, making 2 pieces 36 ins. × $1\frac{3}{4}$ yds.
2. Plucking up pieces of the double silk and using fine string, tie (at random) small circles towards one end and larger circles towards the other end.
   see diagram below
3. Turn material over and make random ties on the other side. Make sure the ties are smaller at one end and larger at the other end.
First Dye
4. When about 40 circles have been tied, dye in Bahama Blue.

5. Wash off surface dye and untie.
Second Tie
6. Repeat 2 and 3, tying completely at random so that some circles overlap the first circles.
Second Dye
7. Dye in Lilac Dye.
8. Wash and untie circles.
Third Tie
9. Repeat 2 and 3, overlapping parts of existing circles.
Third Dye
10. Dye in Purple Vine.
11. Wash off surplus dye.
Fourth Tie
12. Without untying any circles, tie as many more circles as you can possibly fit into the existing spaces, still keeping the pattern of gradual change from large to small circles.
Fourth Dye
13. Dye in Leaf Green Dye.
14. Wash off surplus dye.
15. Untie all circles.
16. Allow material to dry completely, then wash and iron.

continued overleaf

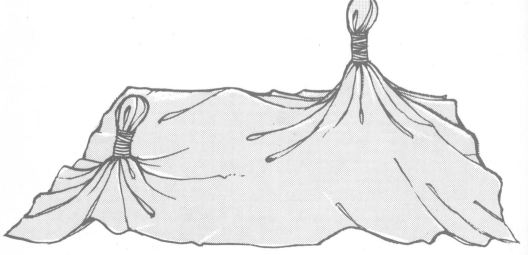

Making Up

A. Place 2 pieces of material together and fold in half lengthwise.

B. On edge opposite selvedges (selvedge is the finished lengthwise edge on each side of the fabric) cut a strip $5\frac{1}{2}$ ins. from the edge and $14\frac{1}{2}$ ins. from the top (the end with the smaller circles).
see diagram 1

C. Cut edge of sleeves.

D. Sew underarms and sides of garment, then back centre seam.

E. Fold back neck edges to 3 ins. in and 12 ins. down.
see diagram 2

Then sew centre seam below V neck.

F. Sew shoulder seams, making sure to take in a wider edge at the front to allow for folded neck edge.

G. Hand sew hem and sleeve edges.

H. Make a long sash from the two strips that were cut away, inserting a light stiffening material in the centre.

SELVEDGE

1

$1\frac{3}{4}$ yds.

$5\frac{1}{2}''$

edge of sleeve

$14\frac{1}{2}''$

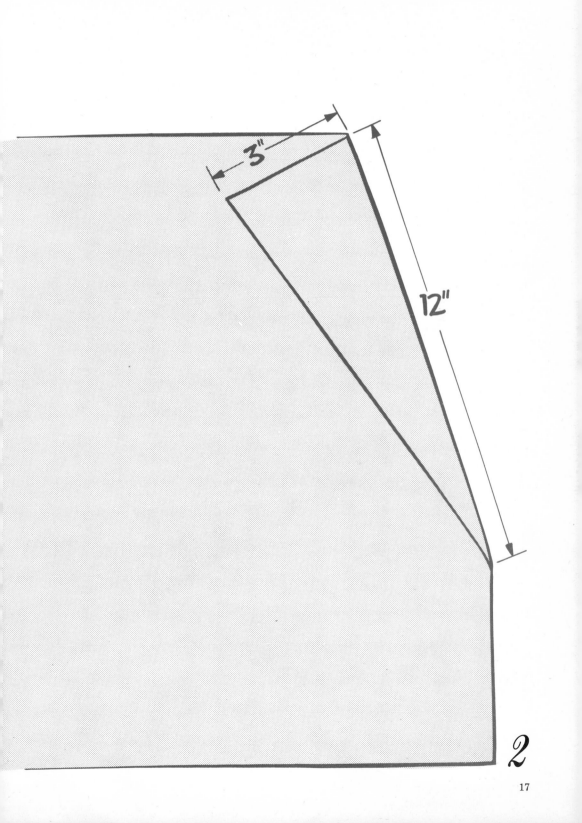

3"

12"

2

Pillow Case

(illustrated on previous page)

Technique
Tied Circles

Materials
1. Cotton sheeting, 60 ins. × 18 ins.
2. Fine string.
Dyes: Bahama Blue, Lilac

Method
First Tie
1. Mark 4 dots as shown.
   see diagram 1
2. Pull up a piece of material from each dot in turn and wind string around from a position about 3½ ins. below dot, up to dot. Tie very tightly at the base.
   see diagram 2

First Dye
3. Dye in Bahama Blue.
4. Wash off surplus dye.
Second Tie
5. Untie first 4 ties.

6. Working in between the two circles in each pair, pick up the two points marked X, as in diagram 1, and wind as in 2 to a depth of about 5 ins.
Second Dye
7. Dye in Lilac Dye.
8. Wash off surplus dye.
9. Untie. Leave to dry, then wash and iron.

Making Up

A. Turn in 1½ in. hem.
B. Follow diagram making sure that the two sets of circles are symmetrically placed on the front of the pillow case. (It is not possible to give measurements here as materials shrink by varying amounts in processing.)
   see diagram 3

C. Reverse and press.

1

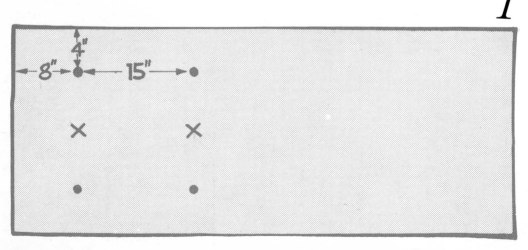

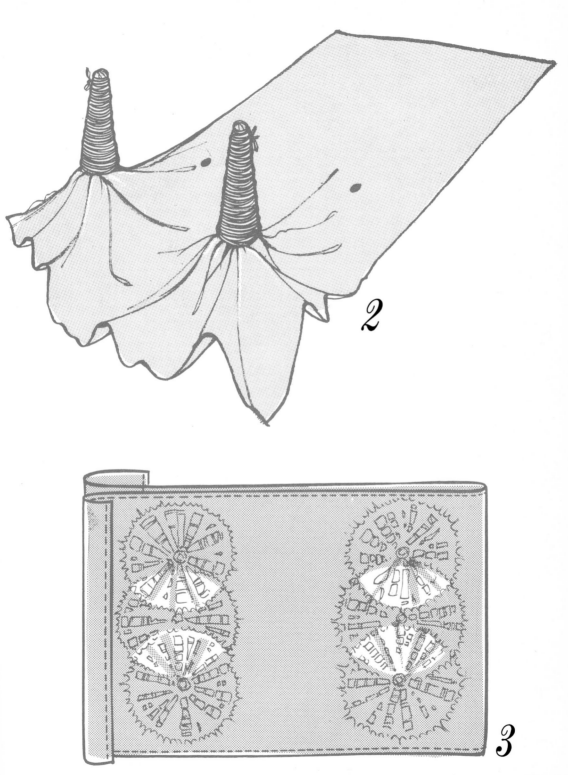

2

3

Hand Towel

Technique
Pleating

Materials
1. One plain white cotton towel.
2. String.
Dye: Purple Vine

Method
First Tie
1. Pleat material across and tie tightly with string at 4 ins. intervals.
First Dye
2. Dye in Purple Vine. Keep material submerged but do not agitate. Retain dye.

3. Wash off surplus dye.
Second Tie
4. Untie all first strings, open up towel, and pleat in the opposite direction to the first pleats.
5. Tie tightly at 4 ins. intervals.
Second Dye
6. Repeat 2 and 3.
7. Dry, untie, wash and tumble dry.

Another method of pleating is to fold your piece of cloth in half, pleat it, and then secure it with pegs.

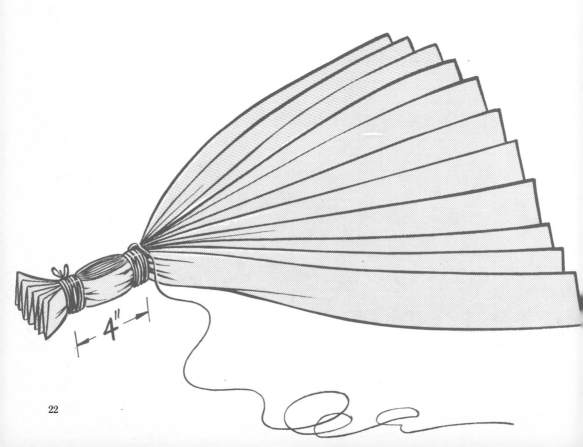

4"

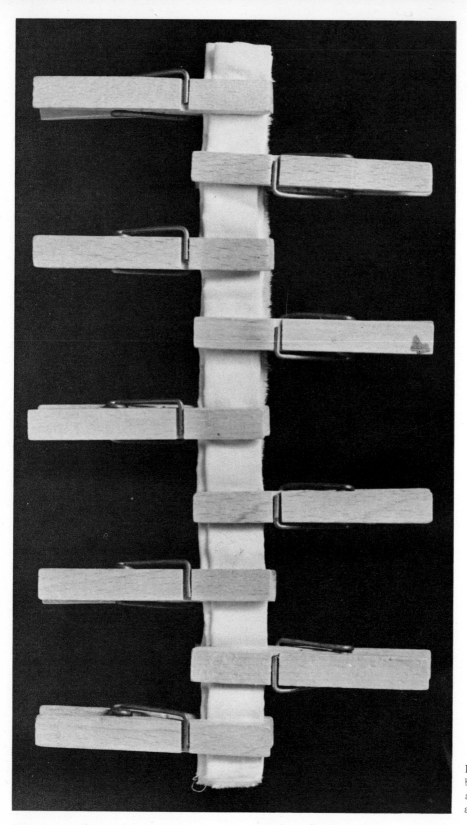

Do not use your
best wooden peg
as they will also
affected by the d

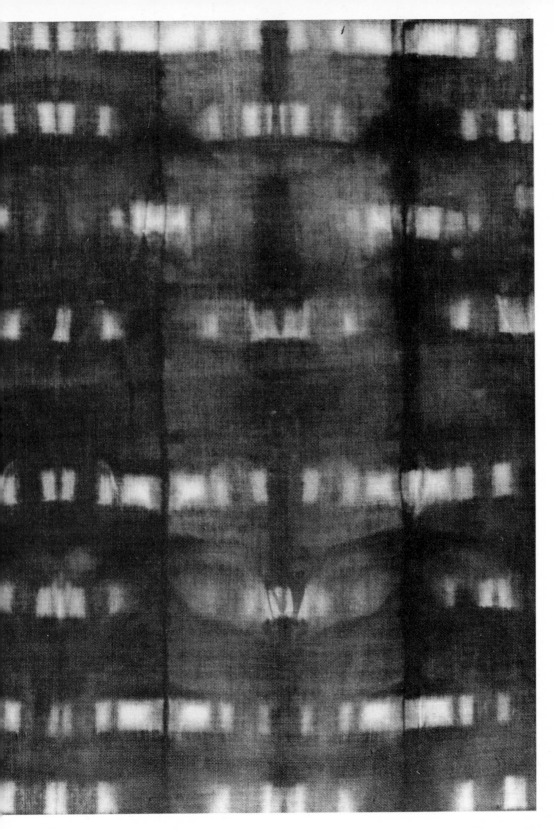

African Shirt

Technique
Pleating

Materials
1. 2 yds. 36 ins. white cotton poplin or other fine cotton.
2. Fine or medium weight string.
Dyes: Tartan Green, Purple Vine

Method
First Tie
1. Fold material in two crosswise to make 36 ins. square.
2. Pleat across material from selvedge to selvedge and tie at intervals of approximately 4 ins. Tie very tightly.
First Dye
3. Dye in Tartan Green, keeping material submerged but without agitating.
4. Wash off surplus dye.
Second Tie
5. Tie tightly with string in between all the first ties.
6. Untie *alternate* first ties.
Second Dye
7. Dye in Purple Vine, keeping material submerged but not agitating.
8. Wash off surplus dye.
9. Dry, untie, wash and iron.

Making Up
A. Cut 12 ins. strip from one end of fabric, then cut that strip in half to make 12 × 18 ins. sleeves.
   see diagram below

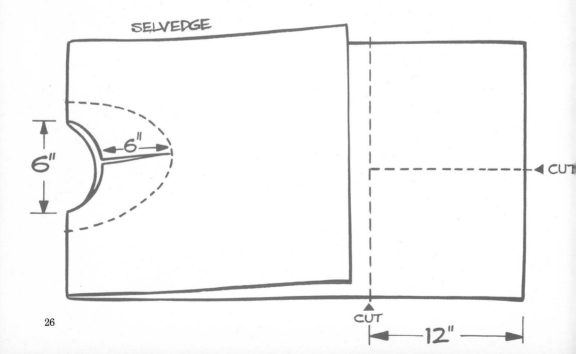

continued from previous page

B. Cut 6 ins. diameter circle in centre of remaining material and a 6 ins. slit down front of shirt.

C. Make facing for neck and slit from any oddment of cotton material.

D. With right side outside, sew facing around neck, then pull through to reverse of fabric.

E. Sew sleeve pieces.

see diagram 1

F. With right sides inside, sew sides and underarms of shirt, leaving a 5 in. slit at waist.

see diagram 2

G. Sew narrow hems along bottom of shirt and sleeves.

H. Turn shirt with right side outside and make parallel rows of stitching around neck and side slits.

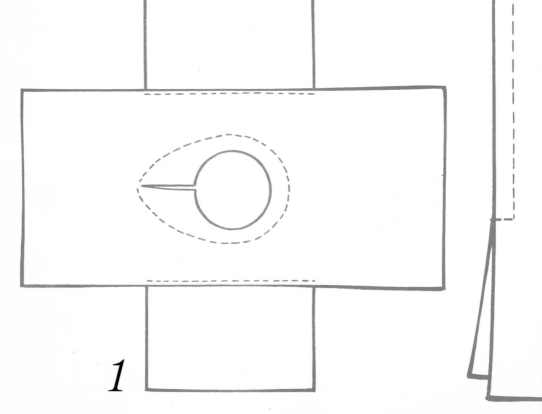

1

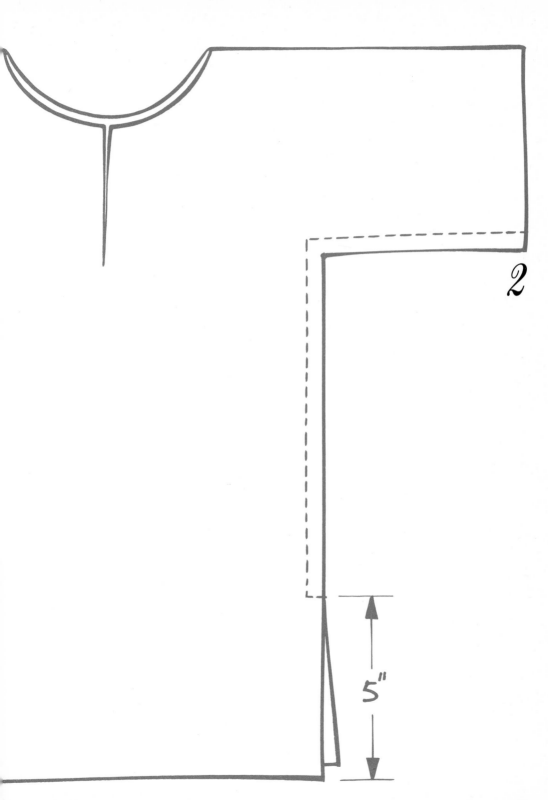

5"

2

Silk Scarf

Technique
Pleating

Materials
1. 1 yd. of 36 ins. white silk.
2. Fine string.
Dyes: Bahama Blue, French Navy

Method

First Tie
1. Fold material in two, bringing selvedges together.
   see diagram 1
2. Fold C D on to A B.
   see diagram 2
3. Fold C D back towards X Y.
4. Fold A B back towards X Y. This will result in a zigzag strip of silk about 4 ins. wide.
   see diagram 3 overleaf

5. Fold the strip diagonally up and down as shown in diagram 4. This will give a fairly solid triangle of approximately 6 ins. × 4 ins. × 4 ins.
   see diagram 4 overleaf
6. Tie very tightly across the 3 corners.
   see diagram 5 overleaf

First Dye
7. Dye in Bahama Blue.

Second Tie
8. Tie on top of first ties, extending farther in each direction. Tie very tightly.

Second Dye
9. Dye in French Navy.
10. Wash off surplus dye.
11. Untie, dry, wash and iron while wet.
12. Hand roll edge of scarf.

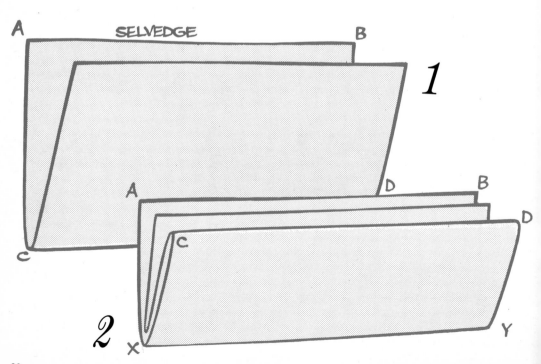

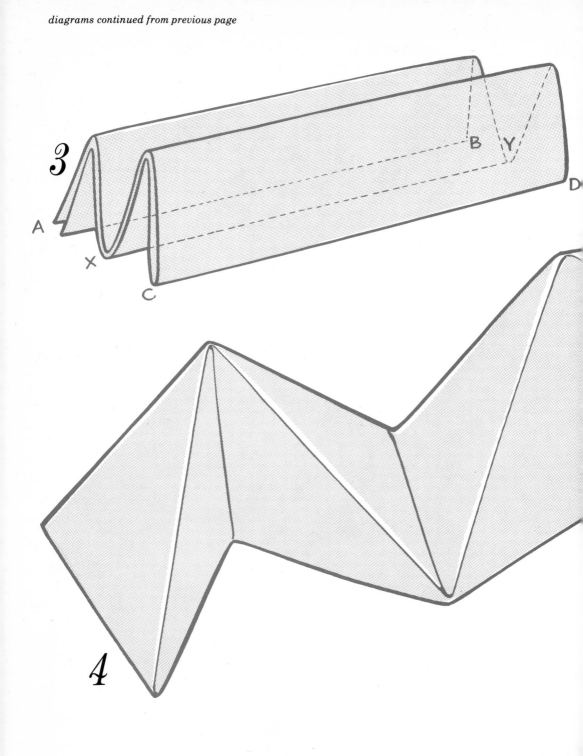

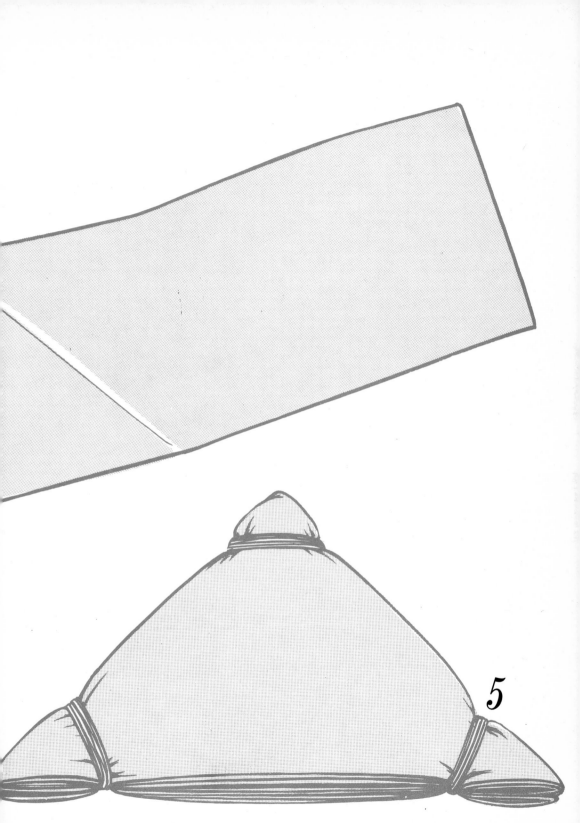

5

Wall Hanging

Technique
Pleating

Materials
1. $\frac{1}{2}$ yd. 36 ins. white cotton.
2. 2 × 18 ins. bamboo rods.
3. 2 eyelets and length of cord.
Dye: Purple Vine

Method

First Tie
1. Pleat in exactly the same way as for the silk scarf (p. 30), but omit the last fold.

First Dye
2. Dye in Purple Vine or any other strong dye or combination of dyes.
3. Dry, untie, iron.

Making Up

A. Sew a narrow hem down the 2 long sides and a 1 in. hem at the top and bottom.
B. Slot one rod through each end; screw eyelets in top rod and thread cord through.

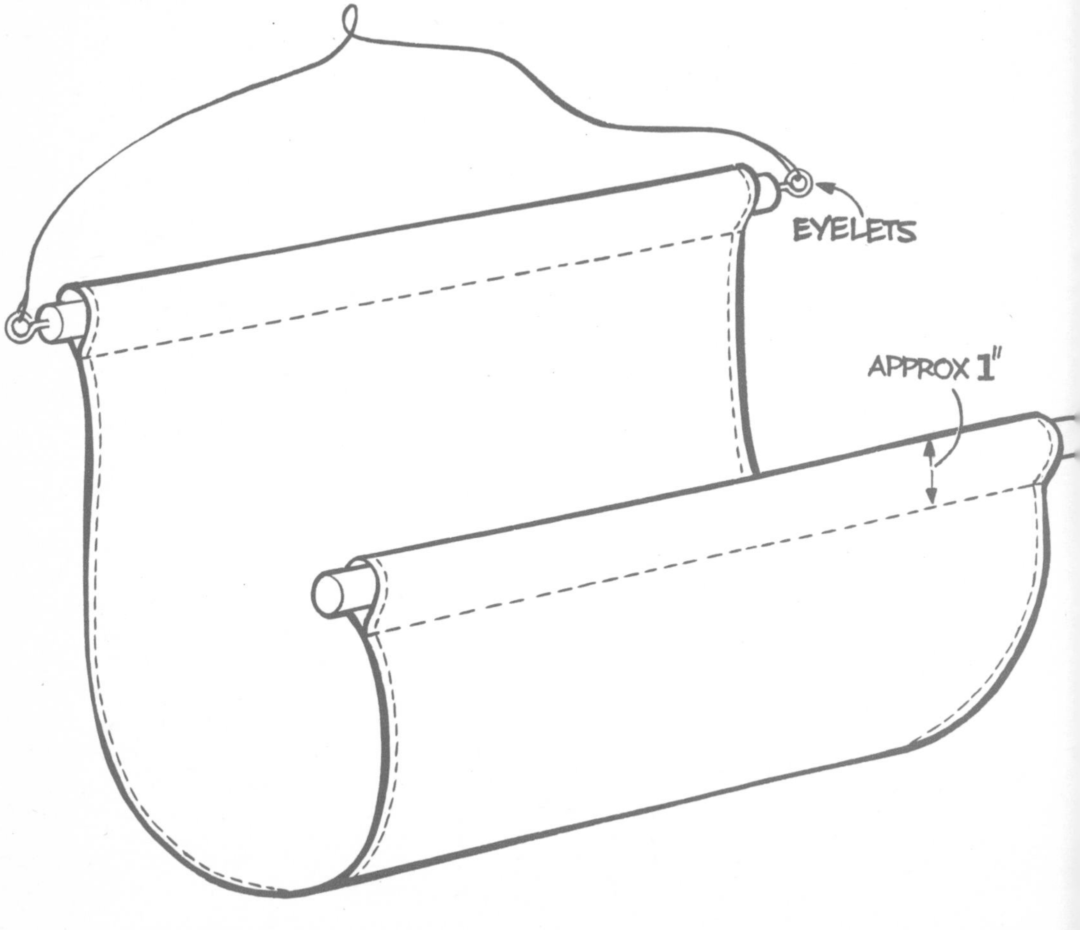

EYELETS

APPROX 1"

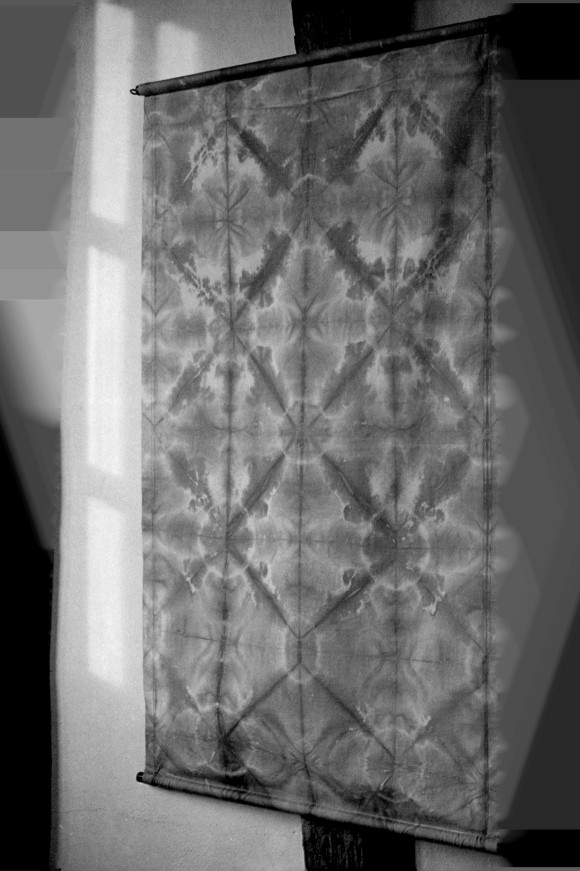

Other Methods of Pleating

Pleating can be used to produce stripes of many different kinds.

A. Cloth folded in half, pleated and open bound with rubber bands.

B. Cloth folded in half, pleated and bound straight with rubber bands.

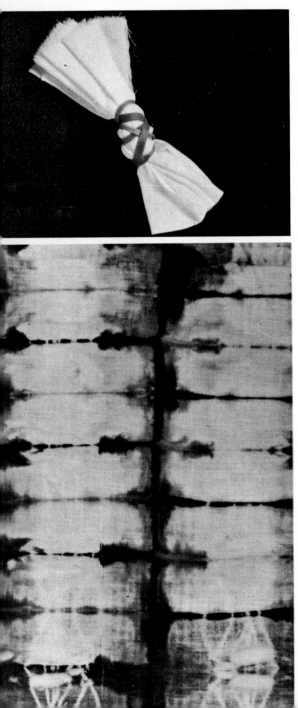

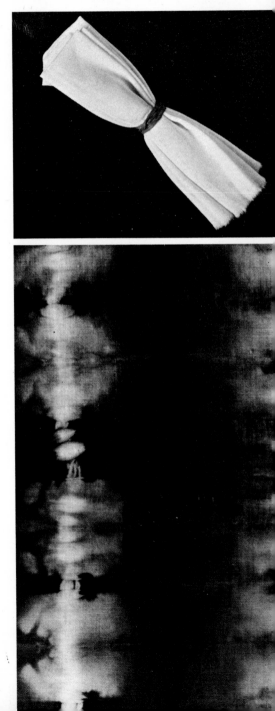

C. Cloth folded in four, pleated and line bound.

D. Cloth folded in six, pleated and line bound.

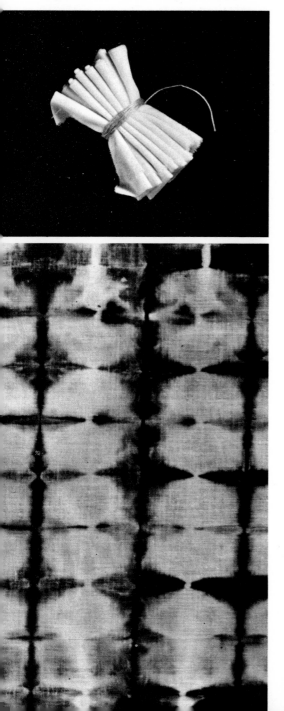

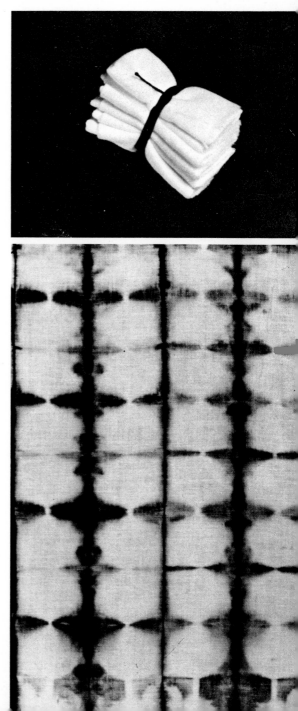

Blouse and Skirt

Technique
Pleating

Materials
1. 9⅓ yds. 36 ins. white cotton
2. 8 in. zip for skirt
3. 6 in. zip for blouse
4. ⅔ yd. skirt stiffening for waistband
5. 1 yd. ½ in. bias binding
The materials and method of patterning allow for the making up of the blouse style to be altered if required.
Dyes: Purple Vine, French Navy

Method

First Tie
1. Cut material as shown in diagram, folding where indicated on dotted lines.
see diagram below

2. Working on each folded piece separately, pleat diagonally at a 45 degree angle and tie tightly with string at 3 ins. intervals.
First Dye
3. When all 5 pieces have been tied, dye in Purple Vine. Make sure that all material is fully covered, but do not agitate.
4. Wash off surplus dye.
Second Tie
5. Tie very tightly again between each of the original ties, then remove the first ties.
Second Dye
6. Dye in French Navy, again keeping all material well covered, but do not agitate.
7. Wash off surplus dye.
8. Allow to dry. Open up material, wash and iron. *continued overleaf*

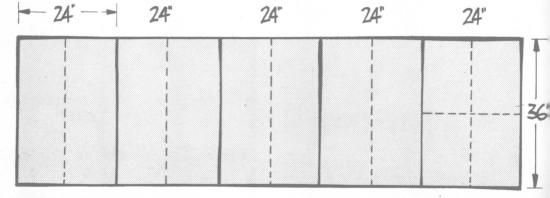

Making Up

Skirt

A. Cut the 4 skirt pieces as shown in diagram 2, being careful to check that the separate pieces are lined up correctly with all of the lines lying in the same direction and the 'V' exactly on the fold.

B. Sew one side seam from 8 ins. below waist to hem.

C. Insert zip.

D. Sew remaining side seams.

E. Sew in waistband and stitch bottom hem to required length.

Blouse

F. Cut blouse as shown in diagram 1 with the 'V' on the fold.

G. Sew dart, then shoulder seam.

H. Sew the 2 waistband pieces in centre, then sew this piece to the bottom of the blouse.

I. Insert 6 in. zip in back of blouse.

J. Sew bias binding around neck edge and back of blouse.

Blouse

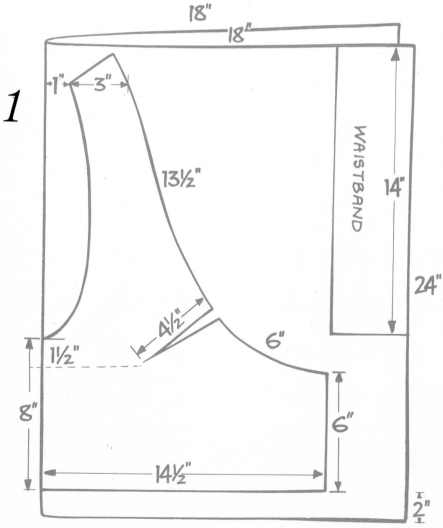

3¼"

8" ZIP

32"

Skirt

2

2½"

Knotting Techniques

The knotting technique has been used for this beautiful sample opposite. Use the design for anything, from a handkerchief to a headscarf.

Method

1. Knot the material according to the diagrams.
2. Dye yellow.
3. Dip large central knot and knots at points in brown dye.

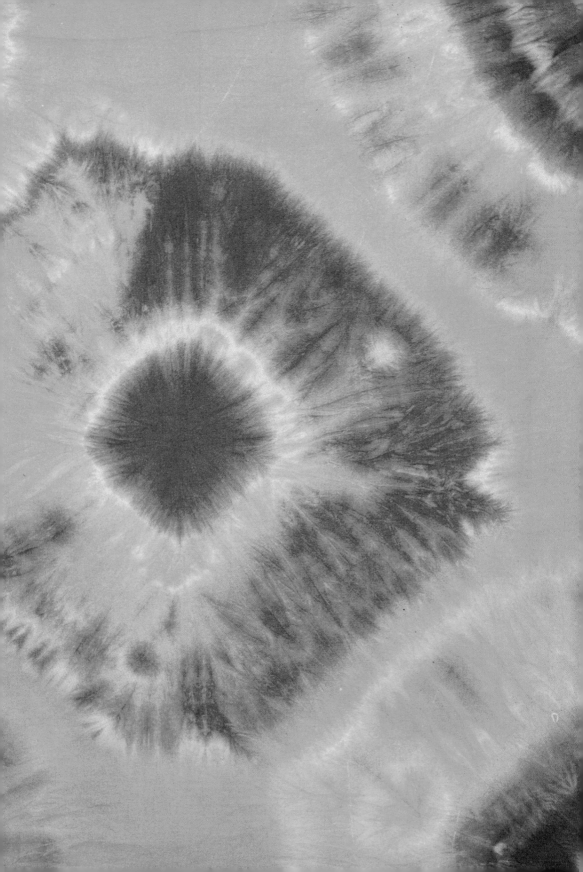

Knotting Techniques

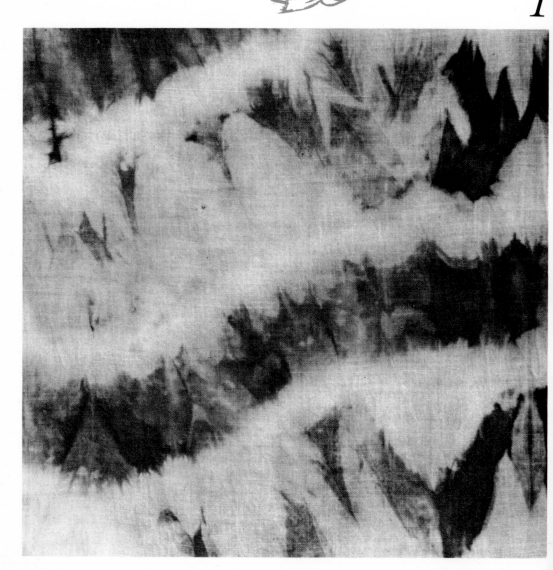

Here you can see other effects obtained by slight variations of the knotting technique.
1. Knotting a length of material with three knots.
2. Knotting a square with a centre knot and four corner knots.

1

2

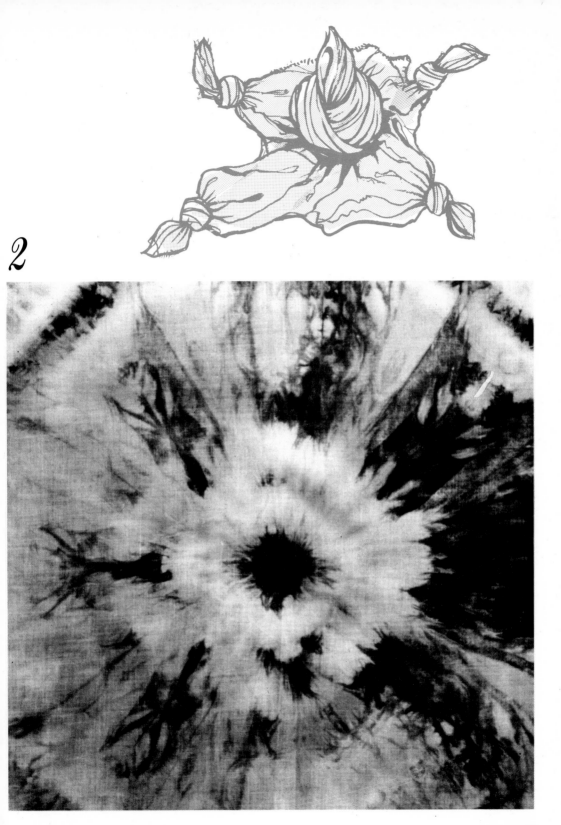

Summer Skirt

Technique
Knotting

Materials
1. 2½ yds. cheesecloth.
2. ¾ yd. 1 in. elastic.
Dyes: Tartan Green, French Navy

Method

First Tie
1. Push selvedges towards centre to make a long thin "rope".
2. Tie a knot in middle of "rope".
   see diagram
3. Leaving about 8 ins. between each knot, tie the whole length.

First Dye
4. Dye in Tartan Green.
5. Wash off surplus dye and untie knots.

Second Tie
6. Tie in spaces between first knots.

Second Dye
7. Dye in French Navy.
8. Wash off surplus dye and untie knots.
9. Leave to dry. Wash again and iron.

Making Up

A. Cut material in two crosswise.
B. Sew side seams.
C. Sew deep hem with double row of stitches at waist and thread through elastic.
D. Sew bottom hem.

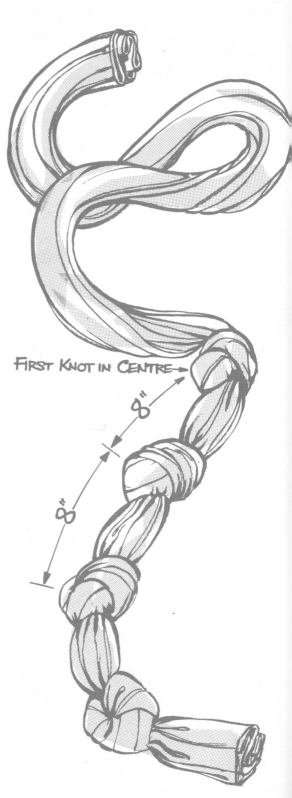

FIRST KNOT IN CENTRE →

8"

8"

Tray Cloth

Technique
Fold and tie

Materials
1. 22 × 14 ins. white cotton.
2. Fine string.

Tying
1. Fold material in two, bringing selvedges together.
   see diagram 1
2. Fold in the same direction as many more times as possible.
3. Tie round in centre several times until the string covers about ¼ inch of material.
4. Tie string round once 2 ins. in from either end.
5. Tie round several times a further 1 inch in from previous ties at either end.
6. Tie string round once centrally between the thick lines.
   see diagram 2
7. Wet the ties under lightly running tap to bring out greater contrast.

Dyeing
8. Dye in a dark blue.

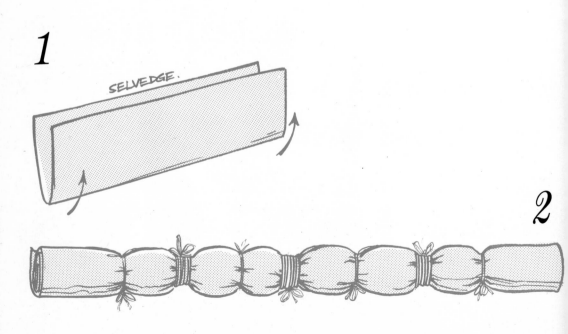

1

SELVEDGE.

2

48

Curtain

Technique
Folding

Materials
1. Required length of 48 in. wide cotton satin material in gold.
2. 50 ins. rufflette tape.
Dyes: Purple Vine, French Navy

Method

First Tie
1. Fold material in 4 zigzags lengthwise.
   see diagram 1
2. Fold in zigzags along the length of the first fold, making squares.
   see diagram 2

3. Tie across in both directions.
   see diagram 3

First Dye
4. Dye in Purple Vine, pulling corners to let dye in.
5. Wash off surplus dye.

Second Tie
6. Add more ties as in 3.

Second Dye
7. Dye in French Navy.
8. Wash off surplus dye.
9. Allow to dry, untie, wash and iron. Turn over top $2\frac{1}{2}$ ins. and sew on rufflette tape. Hem base.

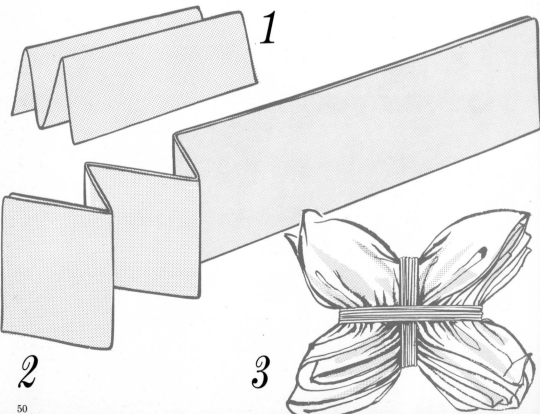

1

2

3

Large Handkerchief

Technique
Fold and tie

Materials
1. 22 × 22 ins. white cotton.
2. Fine string.

Tying
1. Fold the corners into the centre.
   see diagram 1
2. Fold in half.
   see diagram 2
3. Fold in half the other way to form a square.
4. Fold in half again.
5. Fold in half twice more the same way to form a tight roll of material.

6. Tie string round once in centre.
7. Tie string round once ¼ inch in from either end.
8. Tie string round once a further ½ inch in from previous ties at either end.
9. Tie string round several times a further 1½ ins. in from previous ties.
10. Tie string round once centrally between centre tie and previous ties either side.
    see diagram 3
11. For greater contrast, if required, wet the bound areas.

Dyeing
12. Dye in a dark red.

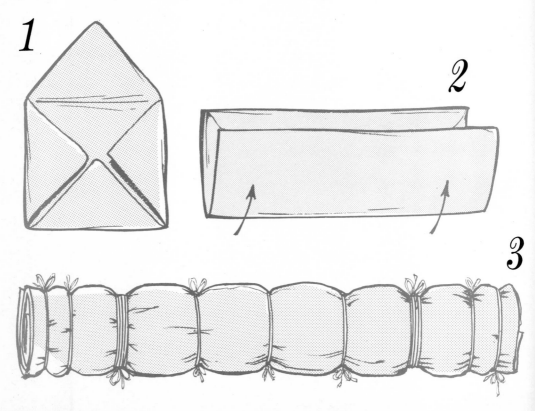

T-Shirt

Technique
Marbling

Materials
1. White cotton T-shirt, larger size than needed.
2. String.

Dyes: Tartan Green, Lilac

Method

First Tie
1. Lay shirt flat and push all edges toward centre in a random fashion.
   see diagram 1

2. Using a long piece of string, wind it round and round the rucked material to make a fairly flat disc, with string tied very tightly.
   see diagram 2

First Dye
3. Dye in Tartan Green.
4. Wash off surplus dye and untie.

Second Tie
5. Repeat 1 and 2.

Second Dye
6. Dye in Lilac.
7. Wash off surplus dye and untie.
8. Allow to dry. Wash and iron.

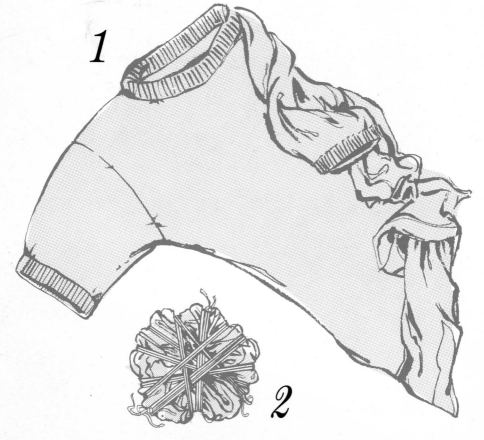

Marbling

Another method of marbling is simply to screw your cloth into a ball and then bind it tightly with string.

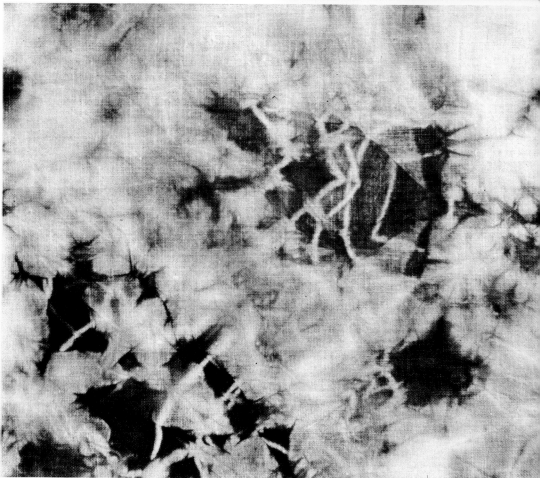

Ruching

For the child's smock that follows we have used a method called ruching. One method of ruching is to roll your cloth around some cord or doubled string, gather and tie tightly.

Child's Smock

Technique
Ruching

Materials
1. $\frac{2}{3}$ yd. of 36 in. cotton.
2. 2 yds. rick-rack braid.
3. 4 fasteners.
Dyes: Tartan Green, French Navy

Method

First Tie
1. Fold material in half over a length of string.
   see diagram 1

2. Fold material in half again over a second piece of string.
   see diagram 2
3. Pull both lengths of string very tight and tie each in a knot.
   see diagram 3 overleaf

First Dye
4. Dye in Tartan Green.
5. Wash off surplus dye.

Second Tie
6. Fold in half. Fold ends into centre over strings. Tie again.
   see diagram 4 overleaf

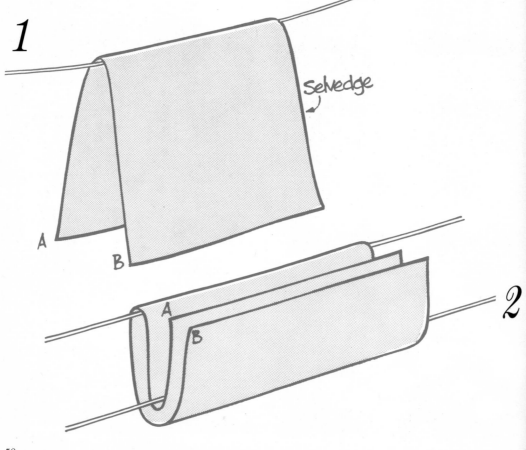

continued from previous page

Second Dye

7. Dye in French Navy.
8. Wash off surplus dye.
9. Untie, dye, wash and iron.

Making Up

A. Fold material in half across, then down.
B. Cut as shown in diagram, making a 3 in. slit down from centre front neck.
C. With right sides inside, sew side seams and one shoulder seam.
D. Sew narrow hems around neck, arms and skirt.
E. Attach fastener to top of neck slit and 3 fasteners to unsewn shoulder.
F. With right side outside, sew rick-rack braid around neck, neck slit, armholes and bottom hem.
   see diagram 5

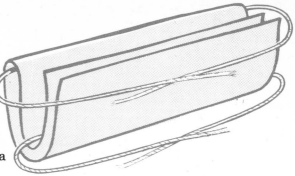

3

4

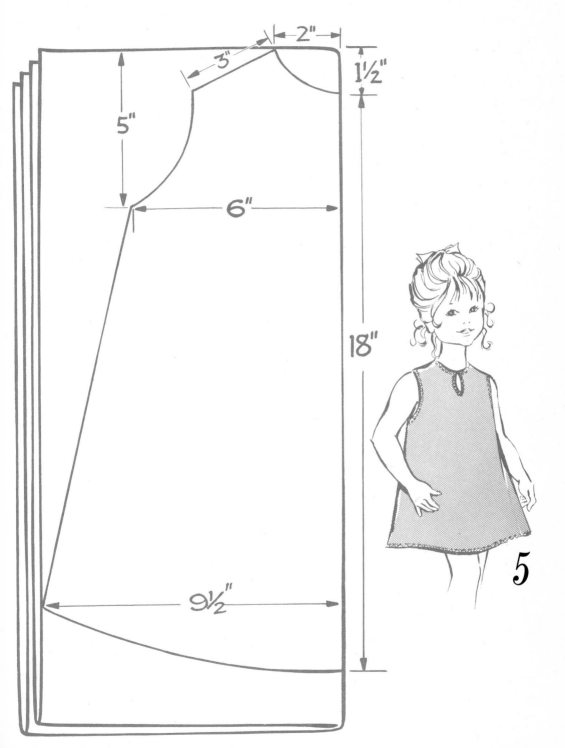

2"

3"

1½"

5"

6"

18"

9½"

5

61

Apron

Technique
Sewing

Materials
1. $\frac{2}{3}$ yd. of 36 in. cotton.
2. 3 yds. 1 in. cotton braid.
3. Linen thread (or double cotton thread).

Dyes: Lilac Blue, Camellia

Method

First Tie
1. Fold material in half with selvedges together.

2. With a pencil, draw 8 lines parallel to the fold at 2 ins. intervals.
   see diagram below
3. Using double thread with a large knot in the end, make a line of running stitches on single material at the fold. Leave end of thread lying free.
4. Fold material again and make separate lines of running stitches along all 8 pencil lines.
5. Draw up threads as tightly as possible. Re-thread needle for each line and finish off lightly.

continued overleaf

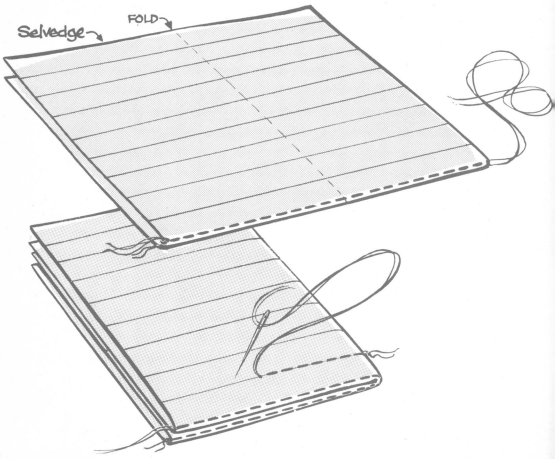

Selvedge

FOLD

continued from previous page

First Dye

6. Dye in Lilac Blue. Submerge fabric but do not agitate.
7. Wash off surplus dye and dry material.

Second Dye

8. Without retying, dye in Camellia. Again submerge but do not agitate.
9. Wash off surplus dye.
10. Dry before untying running stitches.
11. Wash and iron.

Making Up

A. Fold in half lengthwise and cut as shown.
   see diagram 1
B. Sew 1 in. hem at top and bottom and narrow hem down each edge.
C. Stitch braid around curve (doubled) leaving 24 ins. for neck.
   see diagram 2

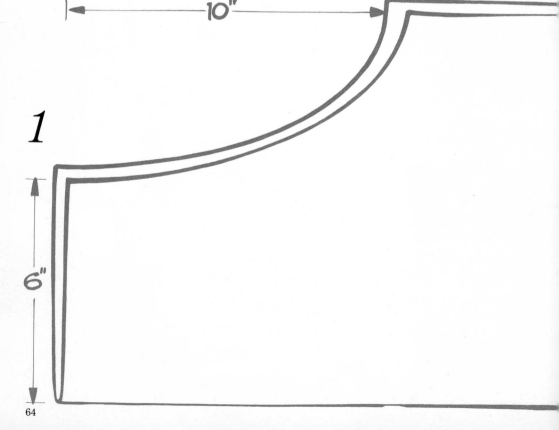

1

10″

6″

2

Sewn Technique

Some other methods of sewing technique are shown here.

1. Sewn spiral, using red dye.
2. Combination of sewn spirals, drawn up running threads and split peas tied into cloth, using blue dye.

Pull up all threads tightly and secure firmly.

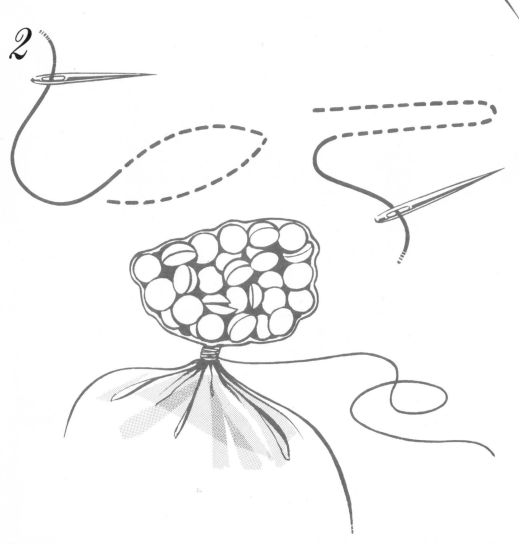

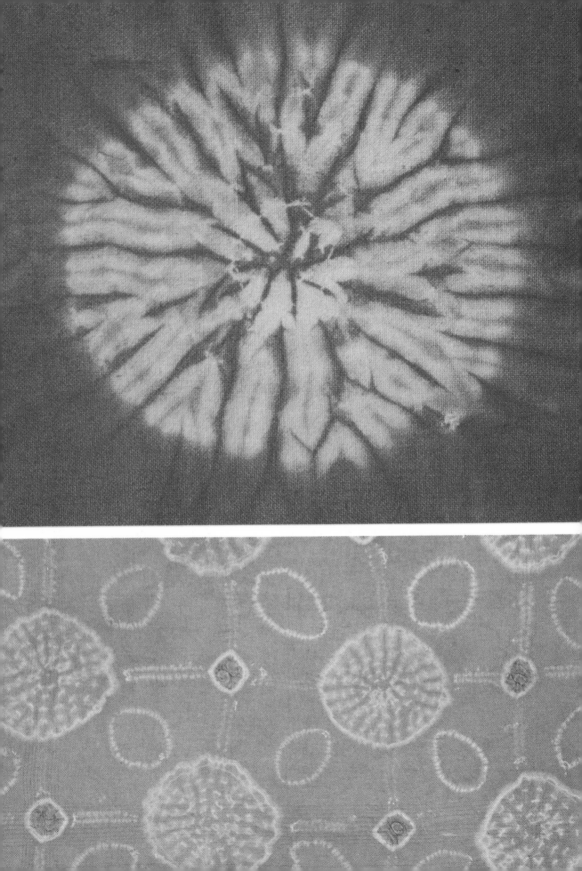

Nine Sample Techniques

Here are nine additional samples of the infinite number of combinations one can achieve with tie-dyeing. You will find a brief description of each below and some helpful diagrams on these pages. Overpage are the finished samples.

1. Folding and dipping, allowing dyes to merge.
2. Folding and dipping avoiding merging.
3. Tie in small stones. Dip yellow, then red.
4. Concertina pleating (warp and weft). Pleat warp and dye pale blue, pleat weft and dye purple. No drying between immersions.
5. Tie in pebbles. Withhold pebbles from dye and immerse in yellow, then pale blue. Dip pebbled cloth in scarlet.
6. Fold and loose tie with heavy cord. Apply lemon and pale blue dye with brush. Give final brush application in desired areas with heavy concentration of canary yellow dye.
7. Fold and dip blue and light brown on basic rose-dyed cloth.
8. Marbling rose, pale blue, turquoise on white.
9. Fold and twist. Dip opposite ends in yellow and blue.

1

2

3

4

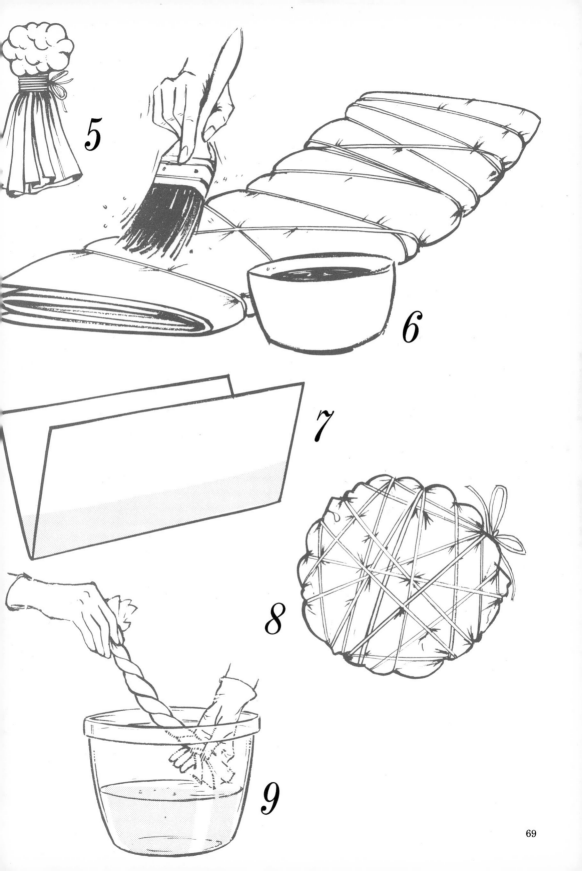

5

6

7

8

9

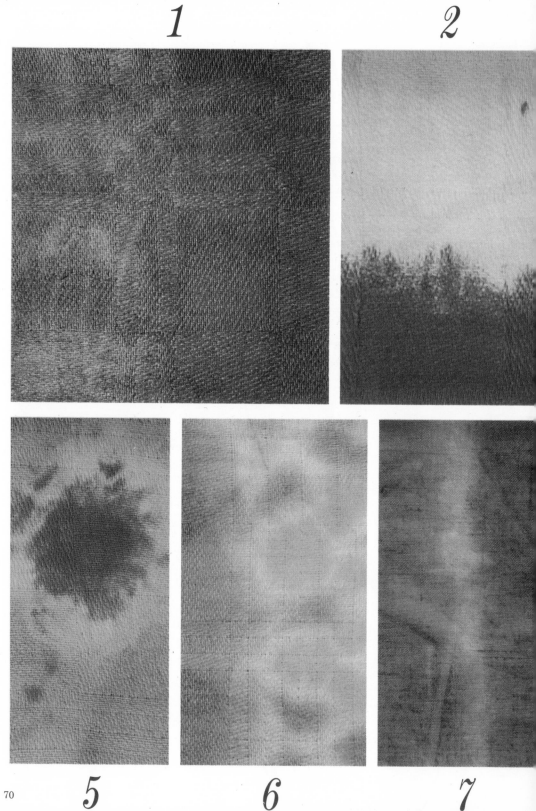

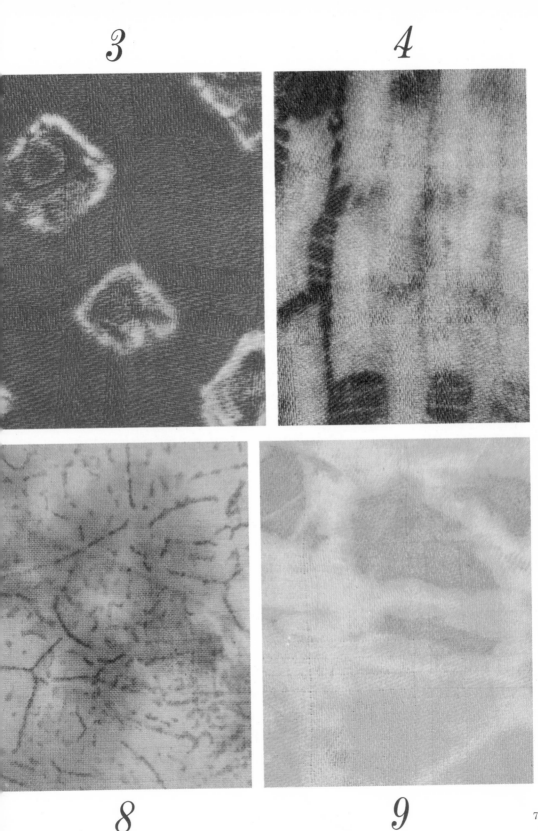

3   4

8   9

71

History of Batik

Batik is an Indonesian word, derived from the word
"titik" or "tik", meaning "a little bit" or "a drop". This
refers to the tiny drops of hot melted wax used on the
design to resist the dye.

The tradition is held to have originated in Java, the most
populated island in Indonesia.

The Persians and Egyptians used a similar technique in
ancient times, but it was the Hindus, who settled in
Indonesia during the 1st and 2nd Centuries A.D., who
developed the art. Batik flourished under the rule of the
East Java kings between the 13th and 16th Centuries. It
was, so to speak, the "property" of the sultans. Later, it was
used by the nobility, and finally, by all of the people.

The art not only survived the collapse of Hindu rule and the
conversion of Indonesia to Islam in the late 16th Century,
but it continues today to influence Indonesian theatre,
puppetry (the 'wayang') and the dance.

Indonesian batik motifs all have special meanings,
derived partly from primitive symbolism but more
influenced by Indian, Chinese and Arabic decorative art.
Still, the Javanese have made batik very much their own.
Patterns may be definite in form (repeated at set intervals
over the material); free (with no fixed repetition); or
unlimited (continuous). The geometric patterns show the
Indonesian influence, while the free forms are based on
Hindu, and sometimes Chinese, designs.

One of the best-known patterns is the parang russak
(similar to a double spiral), which occurs in a variety of
forms. This motif, seen mainly in Java, is permitted only
on the clothing worn by the nobility. There are hundreds
of other symbols used, relating specifically to Indonesian
culture and surroundings. To name just a few, there is the

Dawung, also geometrical in form, resembling the sugar palm tree fruit of the same name; the Garuda, a bird from Hindu mythology and symbol of Indonesia today; and stylized versions of mountains and flames.

Perhaps the best account of the way the Javanese batik is given by Aisjah Soedarsono, from Cilandak (pronounced Chilandak), Indonesia:

"We batik both sides. It's part of the old Javanese philosophy that holds that a person should be the same inside and out. In other words, be honest to himself. The feeling of the Javanese way of life naturally influenced the way batiks are made. But not just their composition.

"During the time you work on batik, you shouldn't talk. Your feelings should be quiet and clear.

"The tjantings (the spelling has now been changed by law to 'canting', pronounced 'chanting') – drawing pens filled with molten wax – must be very clean otherwise you may get stuck as you're drawing. Once you start drawing with a canting, your hand must be nimble, sure and mustn't stop and rest too much once you have begun one of the long, curving batik lines. Once you've finished the drawing on both sides – if possible exactly the same – you go back to the first side and add the myriad little dots and lines which give batik designs their special lightness. After that you do the same on the other side."

Although, in the West, we don't usually batik on both sides, or have the time to spend long peaceful days watching a pattern develop, we can adopt some of the patient Indonesian feeling to our more accelerated Western methods, described and illustrated for the following garments and decorative pieces, which were designed for ease of working and dyeing.

How to Batik

Materials

1. White cloth: choose natural fibre fabrics such as cotton, linen and silk. If cloth feels stiff, wash in boiling water with soap and detergent to remove the finish (starch) and to give material a better affinity to the dye.
2. Wooden frame.
3. Bowls.
4. Jug.
5. Spoons.
6. Wax: 1 part beeswax/4 parts paraffin wax.
7. Solid pan or special wax pot.
8. Heater.
9. Iron.
10. Newspaper.
11. Rubber gloves.
12. Salt.
13. Soda.
14. Drawing pins.
15. Soft pencil.
16. Tjanting, or Canting.
17. Paint brush.
18. Dye.

continued overleaf

Opposite: Detail of a Javanese Batik.

continued from previous page

Method

1. Pin cloth tightly over the frame.
   Draw design onto cloth with soft
   pencil.
2. Heat wax until hazy blue smoke
   appears. Apply wax with canting
   or paint brush to that part of the
   design you do not wish to "take"
   the dye.
3. The size of the canting nozzle varies.
   The "pen" is filled with hot wax.
   (Before using a canting for the first
   time, scribble with it on a remnant,
   just to get the feel of it.) The wax
   will run out of the nozzle very
   quickly and may form a "blob". Just
   continue and make the "blob" into
   part of the design. Keep the canting
   at a steep angle so that the hot
   bowl-like part of the instrument does
   not touch the cloth.
4. When waxing is completed, remove
   the cloth from the frame and crumple
   underneath a cold water tap. The
   cloth should be wet before entering
   the dye to ensure even dyeing. The
   crumple of the cloth cracks the wax,
   giving the effect of streaks of colour
   appearing on a white or coloured
   ground.
   continued overleaf

2

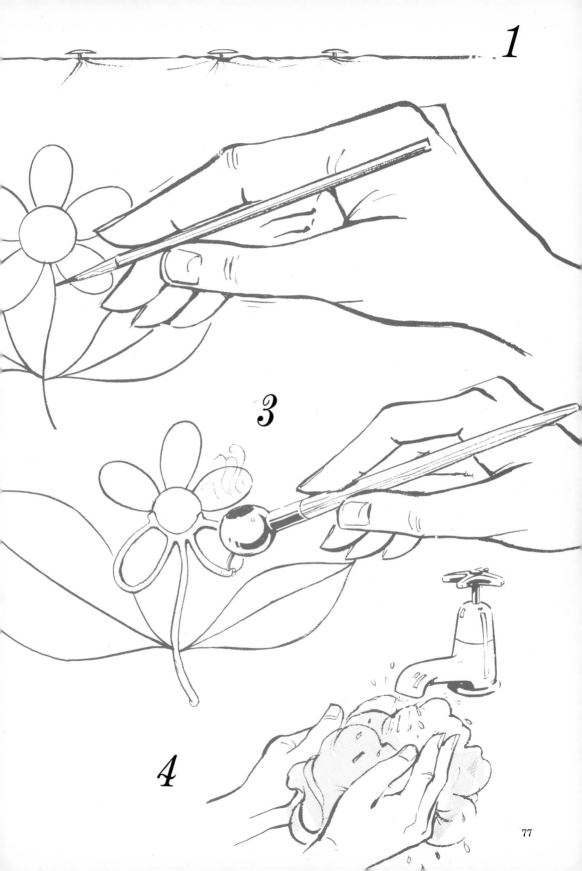

1

3

4

continued from previous page

5. The cloth is ready for the dye.
   Prepare two solutions separately:
   a. The dye and warm-to-hot water
      (see p. 8 for types of dyes, amounts,
      and water temperature, in tie-dye
      section).
   b. Salt, soda and warm-to-hot water.
      (1 pint of water for each container
      of dye. 4 heaped tablespoons of salt
      for each container. 1 heaped
      tablespoon of soda for each
      container.)
   Combine solutions. Immerse cloth
   and keep it moving by stirring with
   spoon so that dyeing is even. When
   dyeing is complete, rinse under cold
   water to remove all excess dye. Rinse
   until water runs clear.
6. Hang cloth to dry away from heat,
   and preferably near a draft or open
   window. When completely dry, the
   cloth is ready for re-waxing.
7. Pin cloth back onto the frame and,
   using a brush or canting, wax new
   areas of the cloth, then re-dye. Now,
   not only will the original areas be
   kept white but some of the recently
   dyed areas will retain their colour.
   So a build-up of shape and colour has
   begun.

7

Enlarging a design

If you wish to enlarge any of the batik designs offered in this book, follow this simple graph method. Or, for a small fee, you can have your design enlarged by a photo enlarging machine.

If you wish to reduce any design, use the same principle but at stage 4 draw your square smaller.

1. Using a ruler and sharp pencil, draw a square or rectangle around the design.

2. Find the centre and draw one vertical line and one horizontal line to form a perfect cross.

3. Divide these again.

Note
The best way to transfer your design onto fabric is to use the same method as for enlarging the design. Draw a large grid faintly onto the fabric and use a soft pencil to copy the design.

4. Draw another square or rectangle, this time to the size required, and divide in the same way.

5. Copy the design square by square.

Table Cover

Materials
White cotton lawn, 37 ins. × 37 ins.
Dyes Café au lait, Sahara Sun,
Nasturtium.

Method

First Waxing
Wax design as indicated on trace
design with brush.
First Dyeing
Immerse in Café au lait. Wash out wax.
Second Waxing
Re-wax with brush by repeating the
design but blocking out whole rings of
colour on white and waxing inside
shapes as indicated. Background is
waxed each time, creating more streaks
of colour.
Second Dyeing
Immerse in Sahara Sun. Wash out wax.
Third Waxing
Re-wax as above, saving some of your
colour and shapes by waxing them,
allowing other parts to become darker
by not waxing.
Third Dyeing
Dye in Nasturtium.

Making Up: Hem round to finish off.

See overleaf trace design for Table Cover

Try this alternative design motif

Use this additional motif as the basis
for another design. Repeat the motif
vertically, horizontally or diagonally
close-set or spaced, as you like, to
build up an overall pattern.

There is no need to follow these desi
too closely. They are intended only a
guides towards achieving the effects
our finished objects. The art of batik
in a free-flowing design that is not
necessarily precise or repetitive.

continued from previous page

First waxing is shown in grey
Second waxing is shown in blue

Headband

Materials

Long piece of plain white cotton fabric, approximately 81 ins. × 5 ins. (Size varies, of course, depending on head size.)

Two or three pieces of fabric may be stitched together.

Dyes Nasturtium, Turquoise, Violet.

Method

First Waxing

Draw design on fabric with soft pencil, repeating the design lengthwise. Apply wax as indicated on trace design for first waxing.

First Dyeing

Immerse in Nasturtium. Rinse in cold water. Dry.

Second Waxing

Apply wax as indicated on trace design. Crack wax gently.

Second Dyeing

Immerse in Turquoise. Dry.

Third Dyeing Re-dye in Violet. Each dye will seep through the cracks in the wax, while the background remains a solid colour. Wash, iron, dry clean.

See overleaf trace design for Headband

Try this alternative design motif

Use this additional motif as the basis for another design. Repeat the motif vertically, horizontally or diagonally, close-set or spaced, as you like, to build up an overall pattern.

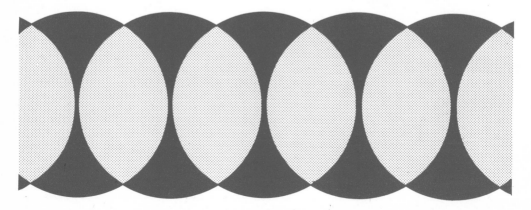

continued from previous page

Cushion

Materials
1. 1 yd. soft, unfinished (no starch) white bleached linen.
2. Stuffed cushion.

Dyes Bahama Blue, Purple Vine.

Method

First Waxing
Paint wax with a medium-size paint brush onto cloth, repeating the design shown, working top to bottom, side to side.

First Dyeing
Immerse in Bahama Blue. Wash out wax, iron and dry clean if necessary.

Second Waxing
Re-wax the same design, but superimpose it on top of previous design, breaking into the pattern by starting cloud effect at a different point. Do not try to copy design exactly but get the general feel of the repeating shapes and lines and create an all-over design.

Second Dyeing
Immerse in Purple Vine. Wash and iron. Dry clean if necessary.

Making Up

Fit material wrong side out over cushion, allowing $\frac{3}{4}$ in. for seams. Sew two sides, leaving one side free. Remove cushion, turn cover right side out and place on cushion again. Join final seam by hand.

See overleaf trace design for Cushion

Try this alternative design motif

Use this additional motif as the basis for another design. Repeat the motif vertically, horizontally or diagonally, close-set or spaced, as you like, to build up an overall pattern.

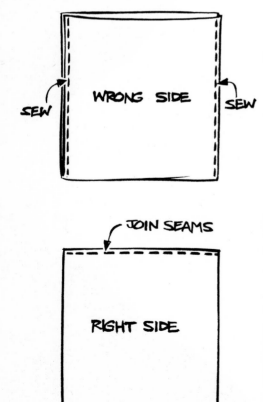

SEW → WRONG SIDE ← SEW

JOIN SEAMS

RIGHT SIDE

First waxing is shown in grey
Second waxing is shown in blue

Hat with Scarf

Materials
1. Straw or fabric hat in a neutral shade or in a colour that will blend with your colour scheme.
2. Jap silk or lining silk for scarf.
Dyes Dawn Pink, Café au lait.

Method

First Waxing
Use a fine paintbrush to wax on "swirly commas".

First Dyeing
Immerse in Dawn Pink. Wash wax out with boiling water. The wax will come out easily from this fine silk. Iron dry.

Second Waxing
Re-wax over and between the previous swirls (the same comma shape) to give an all-over design.

Second Dyeing
Immerse in Café au lait. Wash out wax and iron dry.

See overleaf trace design for Scarf

Try this alternative design motif

Use this additional motif as the basis for another design. Repeat the motif vertically, horizontally or diagonally, close-set or spaced, as you like, to build up an overall pattern.

continued from previous page

First waxing is shown in grey
Second waxing is shown in blue

97

Placemats

Materials

1. Thick linen, 12 ins. × 15 ins. for each mat.
2. ½ inch braid, 54 ins. for each mat.

Dyes Turquoise, Bright Orange (A 26).

Method

First Waxing

Draw design on fabric with soft pencil. Using a canting or fine paint brush, go over areas indicated on trace design with wax.

First Dyeing

Immerse in Turquoise, wash and remove wax. (If wax is cool or dye solution very warm, the dye will seep under the wax and give a tone effect rather than bright white under the waxed areas).

Second Dyeing

Immerse in Bright Orange. Wash, iron.

Making Up

Take up ¼ in. hem.
Sew on braid to finish.

See overleaf trace design for Placemats

Try this alternative design motif

Use this additional motif as the basis for another design. Repeat the motif vertically, horizontally or diagonally, close-set or spaced, as you like, to build up an overall pattern.

Peasant Blouse

Materials
Simple white cotton blouse or smock.
(The one illustrated here was
purchased from a boutique, but the
design shown is suitable for almost
any type of smock, hand-made or
ready made).
Dye Purple Vine.

Method
Draw design at random on blouse with
soft pencil, to give a "sprinkled" effect.

Waxing
Wax with canting or fine brush inside
daisies. If smock has cotton lace
inserted, put wax spots on lace to
resist dye, creating a pattern on lace
areas.

Dyeing
Immerse in Purple Vine. Wash, iron,
dry clean.

See overleaf trace design for Blouse

Try this alternative design motif

Use this additional motif as the basis
for another design. Repeat the motif
vertically, horizontally or diagonally,
close-set or spaced, as you like, to
build up an overall pattern.

Tablecloth

(illustrated on previous page)

Materials
1. White linen, 42 ins. × 44 ins.
2. 172 ins. of 2½ ins. fringe.
Dyes Sahara Sun, Deep Orange (A 27).

Method

First Waxing
Apply design with soft pencil, then go
over with brush and canting for
scribbly pieces.

First Dyeing
Immerse in Sahara Sun. Allow to dry.

Second Waxing
Re-wax, enlarging the design. Re-crack
the wax after it hardens by squeezing
the fabric.

Second Dyeing
Dye in Deep Orange. Wash wax out,
iron and dry clean if necessary.

Making Up

Sew a ¾ in. hem all round.
Sew on fringe.

Large Scarf

Materials
Fine silk or fine cotton, 27 ins. × 27 ins.
Dyes Moon Blue, Radiant Pink,
Nasturtium.

Method
First Waxing
Apply wax with a canting or fine paint
brush as an all-over, non-repetitive
design.
First Dyeing
Immerse in Moon Blue (a grey/blue).

Wash or boil out wax. Iron dry.
Second Waxing
Re-wax new flowers and leaves,
breaking into the Moon Blue ground.
Second Dyeing
Dye Radiant Pink. Wash out wax.
Iron dry.
Third Waxing
Re-wax more flowers over and between
previous design.
Third Dyeing
Immerse in Nasturtium. Wash out wax,
iron dry.

See overleaf trace design for Large Scarf

Try this alternative design motif

Use this additional motif as the basis
for another design. Repeat the motif
vertically, horizontally or diagonally
close-set or spaced, as you like, to
build up an overall pattern.

continued from previous page

First waxing is shown in grey
Second waxing is shown in blue

Long Dress

Materials

Approx. 3 yds. very fine cotton, such as cotton voile.

Dyes Tahiti Rose (pale pink), Dark Pink, Purple Vine.

Method

First Waxing

Apply swirly leafy design using a fine paint brush and a canting.

First Dyeing

Immerse in Tahiti Rose. Wash out wax, iron dry.

Second Waxing

Re-wax more leaf shapes over the top, breaking right through the design.

Second Dyeing

Immerse in Dark Pink.

Third Waxing

Re-wax inside leaves and between them, picking out solid area.

Third Dyeing

Re-dye in Purple Vine. Wash and iron.

Method

To make up the dress, any simple round necked long dress pattern (such as a caftan) can be used. If fullness round neck is required (as shown in diagram 1) allow 4 ins. extra material at centre front when cutting out, then gather to neck size, after which bind neck with 1½ ins. strip of material cut on bias. Insert zip.

To make frilled neck as shown, cut 2 yds. strip of material 3 ins. wide. Hem both sides to leave finished strip 2 ins. wide. Then run three gathering threads through frill. Gather to size of neck and hand stitch to neck line on the right side.

Then with washable silver thread, embroider lines of chain stitch, herringbone and French knots as shown in photograph of finished garment.

If the pattern used has a short sleeve a frill as shown in the photograph can be added. For each frill cut piece of material 20 × 10 ins. on straight of material. Gather to fit bottom of sleeve. Stitch on and hem.

See overleaf trace design for Long Dress

1

2

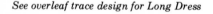

3

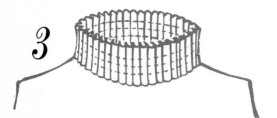

4

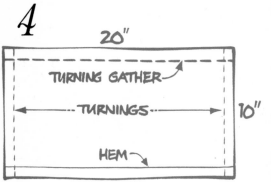

20"

TURNING GATHER

←- - TURNINGS - - → 10"

HEM

5

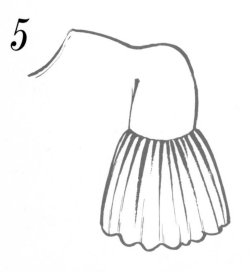

First waxing is shown in grey
Second waxing is shown in blue

Housecoat

Materials

1. 2½ yds. white cotton lawn.
2. Buttons to match.

Dyes Mexican Red, Purple Vine.

Method

Buy a simple pattern, or use the pattern below.

Cut the bodice and sleeves (to be batiked) separately. Dye the skirt parts, which are left a plain colour, with the first dyeing of the bodice and sleeve pieces.

First Waxing

Apply wax with a fine brush or canting to the areas indicated in trace design on bodice and sleeves.

First Dyeing

Dye all pieces in Mexican Red. Allow to dry.

Second Waxing

Wax bodice only, as sleeves and skirt are complete now. Apply wax to shapes between the leaves and grapes and place odd spots of wax in between grapes.

Second Dyeing

Immerse bodice in Purple Vine.

Making Up

Remove all wax. Wash and iron pieces, then sew together and hem. Add buttons and buttonholes. Dry clean. N.B. If cloth is very fine, all wax may come out simply by washing.

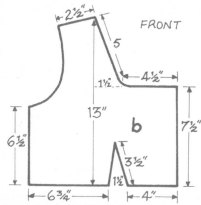

See overleaf trace design for Housecoat

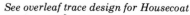

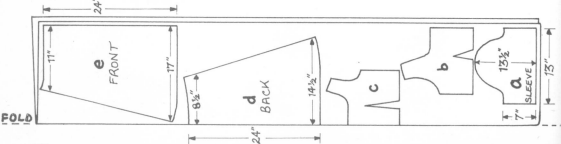

First waxing is shown in grey
Second waxing is shown in blue

Short Skirt

Materials
1. 1¾ yds. cotton poplin.
2. 7 in. zipper.
3. Button to match.
Dye Radiant Pink.

Method
Cut out six panels and stitch together.
(see pattern overleaf).
Cut out waist and secure to panels.
Leave material as one flat piece before
waxing and dyeing.

Waxing
Scribble design with canting over as
many panels as required.
Dyeing
Immerse in Radiant Pink.

Making Up
Wash out wax and iron. Insert zipper.
Join seams, make buttonhole, sew on
button. Dry clean.
More colours and design may be
achieved by re-scribbling over previous
pattern with wax and re-dyeing.

See overleaf trace design for Short Skirt

Try this alternative design motif

Use this additional motif as the basis
for another design. Repeat the motif
vertically, horizontally or diagonally,
close-set or spaced, as you like, to
build up an overall pattern.

continued from previous page

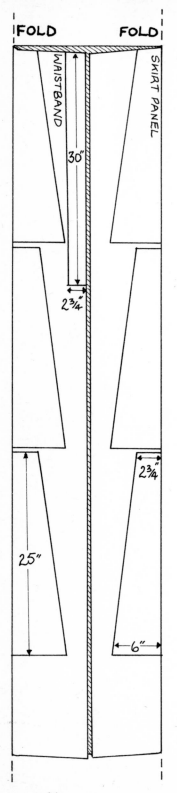

FOLD   FOLD

WAISTBAND

SKIRT PANEL

30"

2¾"

2¾"

25"

6"

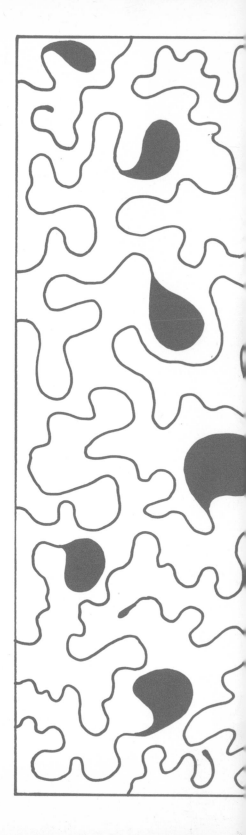

Man's Tie

Material
¾ yd. of white lining silk or any fine silk.
Dyes Bahama Blue, Purple Vine.

Method
Use a tie pattern or an old tie cut into two pieces and pin down on fabric, cut fabric on the bias.

First Waxing
Apply an all-over design with soft pencil, then wax inside areas as indicated on trace design using a canting or paint brush.

First Dyeing
Immerse in Bahama Blue. Wash out wax, iron, dry.

Second Waxing
Re-wax, picking out some solid shapes, working over and between previous design. (See trace design.)

Second Dyeing
Immerse in Purple Vine. Wash or boil out wax. Iron dry.

Making Up
Tie should be lined to hang correctly.

See overleaf trace design for Man's Tie

Try this alternative design motif

Use this additional motif as the basis for another design. Repeat the motif vertically, horizontally or diagonally, close-set or spaced, as you like, to build up an overall pattern.

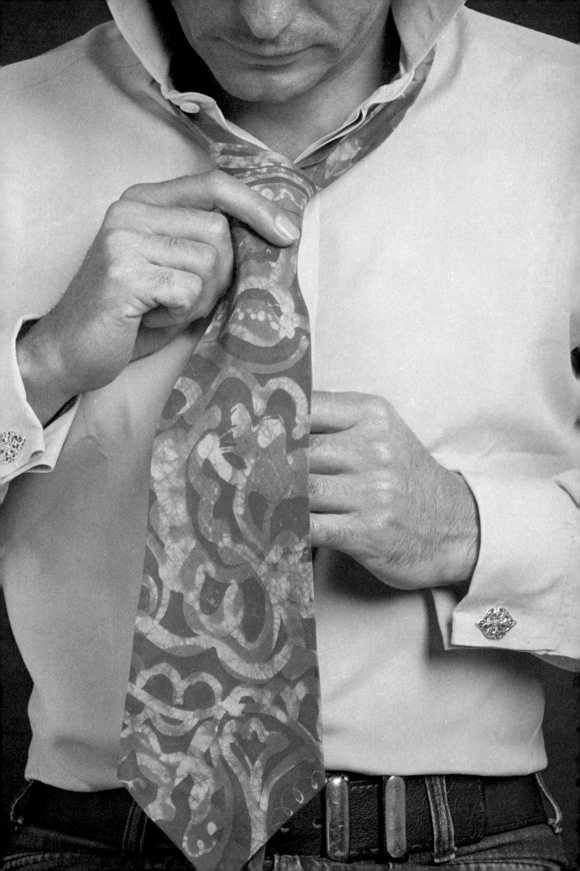

First waxing is shown in grey
Second waxing is shown in blue